Civil War Photographers and Their Work

PORTRAITS OF WAR

George Sullivan

TWENTY-FIRST CENTURY BOOKS   BROOKFIELD, CONNECTICUT

Library of Congress Cataloging-in-Publication Data
Sullivan, George.
Portraits of war: Civil War photographers and their work/George Sullivan.
p.   cm.
Includes bibliographical references and index.
Summary: Presents photographs of the Civil War along with pro-files of the major photographers and descriptions of the difficulties they faced while recording the reality of the conflict.
ISBN 0–7613–3019–4 (lib. bdg.: alk. paper)
1. United States—History—Civil War, 1861–1865—Pictorial Works—Juvenile literature. 2. United States—History—Civil War, 1861–1865—Photography—Juvenile literature.   3. War photogra-phers—United States—Biography—Juvenile literature. [1. United States—History—Civil War, 1861–1865—Pictorial works. 2. War photographers.] I. Title.
E468.7.S85   1998
973.7—DC21   97–49005   CIP   AC

Published by Twenty-First Century Books
A Division of The Millbrook Press, Inc.
2 Old New Milford Road
Brookfield, Connecticut 06804

Contents

Acknowledgments

Not long after he began his career as a photographer in the mid-1840s, Mathew Brady's great ambition became to record the images of every important artist, writer, performer, scientist, clergyman, politician, and military figure of the time—and he succeeded. Then, with the coming of the Civil War in 1861, Brady, still at the height of his fame, sent teams of cameramen into the field, including Alexander Gardner, Timothy O'Sullivan, and James F. Gibson, to photograph such images as battlefields, the war's technology, and fallen soldiers. Brady also acquired the work of other photographers to add to his collection.

In 1874 and 1875, with Brady suffering serious financial woes, the War Department purchased thousands of his Civil War negatives. In addition to the Brady photographs, the collection contained images made under the supervision of the Corps of Engineers and the Quartermaster Department, including photographs made by George N. Barnard in 1864–1865.

The War Department transferred this collection to the National Archives in 1940. The negatives and prints made from them in the 1920s are now to be found at the National Archives' Division of Still Pictures in College Park, Maryland.

In 1943 the Library of Congress purchased another enormous collection of Brady negatives concerned primarily with the Civil War. This collection, which had changed hands six times before being acquired by the Library of Congress, included some two thousand negatives by Alexander Gardner.

Almost all the photographs in this book were selected from those two collections, and the author is most grateful for the opportunity to draw upon them.

Special thanks are due a number of individuals representing these and other cultural institutions, including Mary M. Ison, Maya Keech, and other staff members, Prints and Photographs Division, Library of Congress; James T. Parker, Archival Research International; Diane Ryan, Chicago Historical Society; Mary Panzer, Ann Shumard, and Jeana K. Foley, National Portrait Gallery, Smithsonian Institution; Jennifer Sanchez, the Library Company of Philadelphia; and Theresa Roane, the Valentine Museum, Richmond, VA.

Special thanks are also due Sal Alberti and James Lowe for their warmhearted advice and encouragement while this book was being researched and written, and for their open invitation to use their research facilities; Jeanne Gardner for her early enthusiasm for the project; Larry Schwartz, Archive Photos; Daile Kaplan, Swann Galleries; and Ross Kelbaugh, Historical Graphics.

Photographing the Civil War

When the Civil War erupted in the spring of 1861, photography was only a little more than twenty years old. It was, from a technical standpoint, still in a primitive stage. Nevertheless, during the four years of the war, American cameramen managed to produce more than a million photographs, notable for their variety and technical excellence, for their drama, and, through the scenes of destruction and death that they depict, for their ability to transmit a sense of the war's terrible violence.

Civil War photos "bear witness to real events," according to Alan Trachtenberg in *Reading American Photographs*. "We see the war not as heroic action in a grand style," says Trachtenberg, "but as rotting corpses, shattered trees and rocks, weary soldiers in mud-covered uniforms or lying wounded in field hospitals."[1]

Not all Civil War photographs have these qualities, of course. Many are ordinary—formal group portraits or plain landscape photographs. But those that spoke of the reality of war had the power to both fascinate and shock people of the time. And they still do today.

This book is not a photographic history of the Civil War, nor could it be. In the case of most Civil War battles, no cameramen were present. They simply did not know in advance where battles were going to take place.

What this book does do is examine certain aspects of the war, including some battles, and explain how they were covered photographically. Who took the pictures?

Mathew Brady, whose great ambition was to create a photographic record of the Civil War. This photograph was made from a negative produced by a multilens camera. (National Archives)

When were they taken? What difficulties had to be overcome? What qualities helped to make these photographs "great"?

Thousands of cameramen took photographs during the Civil War. Most of these, however, were studio photographers who made soldier portraits. Of the relatively few who were concerned with the Civil War's battle scenes and important events, Mathew Brady is usually the first photographer mentioned.

In 1861, when the Civil War began, the thirty-eight-year-old Brady reigned as the most noted photographer of the day, with elegant studios in New York and Washington. He was a celebrity photographer. Virtually all the rich and famous of the time had posed for Brady's cameras, including President Abraham Lincoln and several earlier presidents, statesmen, politicians, visiting royalty, theatrical performers, financiers, preachers, military officers, and men and women representing every profession. The *New York Times* called Brady "the prince of photographers."[2]

Brady announced that his great ambition was to create a photographic record of the Civil War. Making war photographs was not a new idea. During America's war with Mexico, from 1846 to 1848, a dozen or more images had been made by unknown cameramen. And during the Crimean War, fought by Great Britain, France, Turkey, and Sardinia against Russia from 1853 to 1856, Roger Fenton, a British cameraman, had made more than a hundred photographs, some quite impressive.

Brady realized that he could not do the actual photography himself. He suffered from failing eyesight as the result of a childhood disease, and by the 1860s the condition had become very serious. Focusing a camera and making an exposure were real problems for him.

Consequently, Brady made plans to hire teams of two photographers each and send them into the field. Each team would be equipped with a canopy-covered, horse-drawn wagon to carry equipment and supplies and serve as a portable darkroom. In this way, Brady hoped that he would be able to produce what he called a "portrait of the war."

While Brady himself visited battlefields only two or three times during the Civil War, his photographers were very active, producing three thousand to four thousand scenes portraying the landscape of the war. "I had men in all parts of the Army, like a rich newspaper," Brady once said. "I spent over $100,000 on my war enterprises." [3]

Brady added to his stock of photographs by purchasing negatives from other photographers or exchanging negatives with them. He also copied other photographers' prints and added them to his collection.

In 1862, Brady published hundreds of these images in several numbered sets. Each print carried a credit line that read "Photo by Brady." But a "Brady photograph" was not always taken by Brady; he did not hesitate to claim credit for photographs taken by others.

Brady never saw himself as a mere photographer. He was like an 1800s version of the Walt Disney Company. Like Disney, Brady's name was his trademark. *The Lion King* and *Hercules* are popular Disney releases. But the general public doesn't know the names of the artists and technical experts who were responsible for these films. So it was with Brady. Only in recent years have people begun to assign credit where credit is due.

Today, Mathew Brady is regarded more as a historian than as a photographer. His plan to document the Civil War, and his dedication in carrying out that plan, helped to produce an invaluable visual record of a critical period in American history.

Of the many photographers hired by Brady, Alexander Gardner was the most notable. A year or two older than Brady, Gardner was born in Scotland and had been

One of Brady's cameramen undoubtedly made this photograph. It pictures Brady (standing at the right) and several of the men who worked for him and an array of their photographic equipment and supplies. Taken at Berlin, Maryland, on October 28, 1862, it depicts (from left to right): Silas Holmes, one of Brady's assistants; a cook named Stephen; E. T. Whitney, a cameraman; H. Hodges, another Brady assistant; a teamster named Jim, and David Woodbury, another cameraman who worked for Brady in the field during most of the Civil War. (Archive Photos)

well educated there. In addition to his knowledge of photography, astronomy, and chemistry, Gardner had studied bookkeeping and accounting. During his life, he was also an author, editor, lecturer, and social reformer.

When Gardner immigrated to the United States in 1856, he was immediately hired by Brady in New York. Two years later, when Brady opened his studio in Washington, D.C., he named Gardner to manage it. Skilled and experienced as a businessman, Gardner helped make the operation a commercial success.

In mid-September of 1862, Gardner gained his first experience as a battlefield photographer. By this time, the industrious Gardner was a member of General George B. McClellan's headquarters staff, attached to the Topographical Engineers with the honorary rank of captain. Gardner's job was to make photographic copies of maps and military documents, which played a vital role in strategic planning.

On September 17, 1862, McClellan's huge army, known as the Army of the Potomac, confronted the Confederate forces of General Robert E. Lee along opposite sides of Antietam Creek in western Maryland. Gardner began photographing the very next day.

The battle of Antietam (Chapter 5) was nothing less than mass slaughter. It is called "America's Bloodiest Day."

Gardner's photographs were unlike any that had been seen before. They depicted both Federal and Confederate dead, young corpses strewn about the battlefield or gathered in neat rows for burial.

Within a few weeks after the battle, Brady exhibited Gardner's Antietam photographs at his gallery in New York. When they were written about in the newspapers, they were identified as the work of Mathew Brady.

Late in 1862, Gardner quit his job as manager of Brady's Washington studio to go into business for himself. Brady's carelessness and indifference about crediting photographs that were published under his name are often cited as factors in Gardner's decision to leave.

The next year, Gardner opened his own photography studio in Washington and hired several of the photographers who had worked with him at Brady's.

Gardner was in Washington supervising the operation of his studio when he learned that the Army of the Potomac was on the move, pursuing Lee's army, which was marching through the Shenandoah Valley, thrusting toward Pennsylvania. The two armies would meet near

Gettysburg, Pennsylvania, in what is considered one of the decisive battles of the war.

Gardner, along with two other of the Civil War's most highly acclaimed photographers, Timothy O'Sullivan and James F. Gibson, rushed to Gettysburg, arriving in time to photograph the battlefield dead and the destruction that resulted from the fighting. Mathew Brady and his camera operators were at Gettysburg, too (Chapter 7).

Of the several thousand photographs taken by Brady's cameramen, by Gardner, O'Sullivan, Gibson, and by the scores of other photographers who sought to cover the war, most portray activities behind the battle lines. There are no photographs of armies actually clashing in battle, cavalry charges, or soldiers on the attack or hastily retreating. There are no "action" photographs.

This is because the technology of the time greatly limited what a camera could accomplish.

In today's camera, light passes through the lens to strike film that unrolls and slides behind a mechanical shutter. To take a picture, the photographer simply points and shoots.

In the 1860s, however, taking a picture was a very difficult process. The average person had neither the knowledge nor the skill to operate a camera.

When visiting battle zones, Brady liked to have his picture taken. Here he poses with General Ambrose E. Burnside at Cold Harbor, Virginia, in June 1864. Burnside seems to be much more occupied with his newspaper than with Brady, and probably didn't realize that he was being photographed. (Library of Congress)

A photographer of the Civil War period had to record each image on a rectangle of glass, often 8 by 10 inches in size. This meant that he had to have on hand a large supply of glass plates, which had to be stored in dustproof boxes.

In making a photograph, the photographer used what was called a wet-collodion process.[5] This involved first coating the glass plate with collodion, a smelly, sticky liquid. The collodion had to cover the glass evenly from one edge to the other.

Then, before the collodion dried, the glass plate had to be immersed in a bath of silver nitrate for three to five minutes. All of this had to be done in a darkroom lit only by red or amber light.

The sensitized plate was then placed in a special holder that enabled the photographer to carry it to the camera without exposing it to light. The big camera, about the size of a microwave oven, had already been mounted on a tripod, aimed at the subject, and focused.

The glass plate was then inserted into the camera. To make a picture, the photographer uncapped the lens for five to thirty seconds, depending on the object being photographed and the amount of available sunlight.

The long exposure times meant that any movement

would cause a blur. A soldier on the run or a speeding locomotive would be recorded as a ghostlike image. For that reason, photographers made no effort to record action.

After the exposure had been made, the photographer returned to the darkroom with the plate to develop it before it dried. If it did dry, it was ruined.

To carry their cameras and chemicals, and to provide the conditions they needed to prepare the glass plate and develop it, Civil War photographers built canvas-covered darkrooms in wagons. Mathew Brady converted horse-drawn army ambulances of the day into traveling darkrooms.

Despite the difficult nature of the process and the hardships under which they worked, Civil War photographers managed to produce a remarkable body of photographs. Those presented in this book were selected chiefly from the many thousands of "Brady photographs" that eventually found a home in the National Archives, the Library of Congress, the National Portrait Gallery, and private collections. Even by current standards, many rank as powerful and expressive images.

The First Shots

On the morning of February 8, 1861, more than two months before the first shots were fired in the Civil War, forty-one-year-old George S. Cook, a shrewd and successful Charleston, South Carolina, photographer, loaded his heavy camera, a supply of glass plates, and the chemicals he was going to need that day into a small rowboat. With the help of an assistant, Cook then rowed out to Fort Sumter, a five-sided brick stronghold with walls 40 feet high that had been built on an artificial island near the mouth of the Charleston harbor.

It was a time of great tension in Charleston. The previous December the state of South Carolina had passed an "ordinance of secession" that proclaimed the state's separation from the United States of America. Six other states seceded from the Union during the next two months.

Abraham Lincoln would not accept the idea of a Southern Confederacy. No state had the right to leave the Union, he believed.

Lincoln turned a deaf ear to demands from Southerners that the Federal government abandon forts and arsenals within Confederate states. When he was inaugurated in Washington on March 4, 1861, Lincoln warned that he would do all in his power to "hold, occupy and possess" all places and property belonging to the Federal government.[1] Lincoln was referring mainly to Fort Sumter.

Fort Sumter was commanded by Major Robert Anderson, a regular army artillery officer who had been wounded in the Mexican War and given command of the

Major Robert Anderson, commanding officer of Fort Sumter, the North's first war hero. Anderson and his men endured 34 hours of bombardment from Confederate guns before surrendering the fort. This photograph of Anderson, taken by George S. Cook on February 8, 1861, more than two months before the shelling began, sold by the thousands to hero-worshipping Northerners. (Library of Congress)

defenses of Charleston in 1860. Despite his Kentucky roots and proslavery convictions, Major Anderson was thoroughly loyal to the Union.

George S. Cook's mission that February morning was to photograph Major Anderson. Thomas Faris, a New York photographer, had requested Anderson's portrait. And Cook realized that there was a profit to be made here, that many Northerners would be eager to buy photographs of the man who, because of his defiance, was fast becoming a great Union hero.

As Cook's heavily laden boat neared Fort Sumter, he could see the cannons that Confederate militia companies had mounted on the beaches of the three islands near the fort. Thousands of Confederate troops occupied encampments around the harbor.

When Cook's boat arrived, the gates of the island fortress swung open, and he and his assistant were admitted (despite a suggestion by one of Anderson's aides that they might be Confederate spies). The two men quickly set up a small darkroom, prepared the glass plates, and mounted the big camera on a tripod. Then Major Anderson and his staff posed for several photographs.

For the three-quarter-length portrait that Cook made, Major Anderson wore a dress uniform with ornamental shoulder pieces, called epaulets. He stood stern-faced, his right hand inside his buttoned jacket. (Many Civil War officers posed in this manner, as Napoleon I, the renowned French general and, later, emperor, had done many years before.)

Once back at his studio, Cook developed the glass plates and made prints. A few days later, the *Charleston Daily Courier* invited local citizens "to call at the rooms of that finished sun-artist, Mr. George S. Cook, [where] they will see the commandant of that post just as he is."[2]

Cook sent negatives of his pictures to the E. & H. T. Anthony Company of New York, a firm that published and distributed photographic images. Mathew Brady was their major client.

The Anthonys mass-produced Cook's image of Major Anderson as a *carte de visite*, a sepia-toned photograph mounted on stiff cardboard. At 2 ½ by 4 inches, the *carte de visite* was a bit larger than a modern plastic credit card.

Cartes de visite, which usually featured celebrities of the time but also scenic views and reproductions of works of art, were produced by the millions during the 1860s. Families often collected *cartes de visite* in albums. During March 1861, the Anthonys made prints of the Anderson portrait at the rate of a thousand a day for sale to hero-worshipping Northerners.[3]

On April 12, 1861, Cook and the residents of Charleston awoke to the sound of Confederate guns. While many Union military posts in communities throughout the South had surrendered to home guard or militia units, Major Anderson showed no sign that he was willing to give up Fort Sumter. The bombardment was the Confederacy's response. It kept on throughout the day.

At night, the Confederates pounded the fort with mortar fire. The next day, fires were raging inside the walls of the fort, and the flagstaff had been shot away. Major Anderson realized that he had no choice but to surrender.

Without question, the attack on Fort Sumter was an act of war. President Lincoln responded by calling upon the states for 75,000 volunteers to serve the Federal government as soldiers. With that, four other states left the Union to join the Confederacy.

Now there could be no turning back. The conflict between North and South would be decided by opposing armies.

During the Civil War, the most noted photographers represented the North. Mathew Brady, Alexander Gardner, and dozens of others maintained their headquarters in or near Washington, D.C. When they went into the field, it was with Union forces.

Photography in the Confederacy was limited mainly to studio portraits of government officials or military figures. This was largely because photographic chemicals, plates,

cameras, and other photography equipment came from suppliers in New York and Philadelphia. To reach Southern cameramen, these supplies had to be shipped aboard vessels that could slip past the blockade that had been established by Federal warships. Consequently, photographers in the South had to use their equipment sparingly.

Cook was one Southern-based photographer who managed to get supplies throughout most of the war. As a result, the astute Cook, working in South Carolina, a Confederate state, was able to produce a wide range of notable Civil War images.

After April 13, 1861, the day that General Anderson surrendered Fort Sumter, Charleston photographers visited the site. This panoramic view, made from three separate images, was taken by James M. Osburn and F. F. Durbec, who operated a "Photographic Mart" on King Street in Charleston. (Library of Congress)

❧ ❧❧ ❧

George S. Cook was born in Stratford, Connecticut, on February 23, 1819.[4] An infant when both of his parents died, Cook was raised by his grandmother in Newark, New Jersey.

At fourteen, Cook left home and headed west. After several years of travel, he arrived in New Orleans. There he took up the profession of portrait painter. By 1845, at the age of twenty-six, he had mastered the art of the daguerreotype, an early photographic process.

Cook realized that as a skilled daguerreotypist he could work anywhere he wanted. After he returned to Newark in 1846 and got married, he and his wife traveled extensively through the South. Cook set up studios in several cities and practiced his craft, selling daguerreotype portraits to local residents.

The Cooks, now the parents of a girl and a boy, settled in Charleston in 1849.[5] Cook opened a gallery and became one of Charleston's leading citizens.

Once his studio in Charleston was operating smoothly, Cook often traveled with his wife and children to New Jersey to visit relatives. The trips north enabled Cook to become friendly with Mathew Brady, the fore-most photographer of the time, and Edward Anthony, an important supplier of photographic equipment and supplies. In 1851, when Brady and his wife left New York for a tour of Europe, he called upon Cook to manage his studio at 204 Broadway.

Cook later operated his own studio in New York as well as studios in Chicago and Philadelphia. But he was forced to close down these operations and return to Charleston and concentrate on his business activities there as the conflict between the North and South deepened.

Cook's hugely successful portrait of Major Anderson was merely the first of many memorable Civil War photographs that he took. After the bombardment of Sumter had ended and Major Anderson and his men had left, Cook returned to the fort. He took photographs of the destruction wrought by Confederate guns, the young Southerners assigned to guard duty, and South Carolina's governor inspecting the fort's cannons.

Cook visited nearby camps, where he made individual portraits of soldiers and photographed troops in formation. General P. G. T. Beauregard called upon Cook to make photographic reproductions of maps and drawings of fortifications for distribution to members of his staff.

During 1861 and 1862, Cook not only continued to receive photographic supplies from the North for his own use, but he also accumulated surplus material that he sold to other photographers.

In 1863, with many more Union ships involved, the blockade became highly effective. But Cook still managed to get photographic supplies. He did so by purchasing shares of stock in blockade runners, sleek ships that were capable of slipping past the slower-moving ironclad Union vessels used to enforce the blockade. Cook was able to get the much-needed supplies and also earned profits when such vessels put up for sale the sugar, coffee, soap, salt, and other scarce items that they smuggled past the Union blockaders.

During the early years of the war, Charleston was a vital port for blockade runners. In April 1863, the Union sought to end the city's role as a safe haven by sending a

When South Carolina governor Francis Pickens (center) and other state officials visited Fort Sumter following Anderson's surrender, Cook was there to record the event. The artillery piece in the foreground, trained on the city of Charleston, is a columbiad, a bronze cannon capable of firing a 10-inch shot about 3 miles.
(Valentine Museum)

battleship and eight other armored warships, called monitors, to bombard Fort Sumter. The attack was driven off. But in September of that year, the Federal fleet returned and began hammering the fort again.

Cook was at Fort Sumter as shells from the ironclads rained down. When he set up his camera on one of Sumter's brick walls, Federal gunners directed their fire toward him. A shell flew by within a few feet of where he was standing.

Later, an explosive charge went off in front of Cook's lens, enabling him to record photography's first picture of a bursting shell.

With Fort Sumter in Confederate hands, a fleet of Union warships attacked early in September 1863. Visiting the fort during the assault, Cook caught this striking picture of an exploding shell. Afterward, a Charleston newspaper praised Cook for risking his life to secure evidence ". . . to show future generations what Southern troops can endure." (Library of Congress)

After Cook had processed his photographs and placed the prints on sale, the *Charleston Daily Courier* hailed him for his "bold feat," declaring it to be "one of the most remarkable acts . . . ever recorded in the history of the war."

On September 8, 1863, after Union ships had been hammering Fort Sumter for several weeks, Cook made this dramatic photograph. It pictures the ruins of the fort's eastern barracks. Two Confederate soldiers pose atop the chimney of the barracks' bake oven. (Library of Congress)

Another photograph made by Cook on September 8, 1863, shows the effects of the bombardment. That day, Federal gunners sought to widen the gap that had been created in the fort's thick walls. (Library of Congress)

nterior Fort Sumter 1865

To shore up Fort Sumter's walls, hundreds of cylinder-shaped, open-ended baskets made of the woven branches of trees or shrubs were constructed. Gabions, as they were called, were filled with earth and stacked in neat rows. Cook made this photograph during one of his visits to Sumter. (Valentine Museum)

Cook and his assistant were praised as heroes who had risked "their lives for the purpose of securing a heirloom . . . to show future generations what Southern troops can endure."[6]

Although Sumter lay in ruins and some Charleston homes had been destroyed, the fort's guns had been successful in driving off the enemy ships. But Cook felt certain that the Union navy had not given up, that ships would return to attack Sumter and Charleston again.

Cook decided for reasons of safety to move his family to Columbia in the central part of South Carolina. By early 1864 the Cook family was established in its new home, and Cook had opened a studio in Columbia.

But tragedy soon hit the Cook family. Cook's wife, after a long, painful illness, died in April 1864. Less than a year later, in February 1865, Federal troops under the command of General William T. Sherman entered Columbia. Fire broke out and ravaged more than half the city; Cook's studio, including his camera, photographs, and records, were destroyed.

Once the war was over, however, Cook was quick to rebound. He returned to Charleston, remarried, and opened a new gallery, which was soon prospering.

In 1873, Cook purchased a studio in New York City, but it was unprofitable, and he closed it the next year. Several years after, Cook invested in a Richmond, Virginia, studio. There he enjoyed almost overnight success. He eventually closed down operations in Charleston in favor of his studio on Richmond's Main Street. Cook died in 1902 at the age of eighty two.[7]

"Throughout his life he possessed a passion for his work," historian Jack C. Ramsay said of Cook. "Although information recorded by his descendants pictured him as a man who loved and was loved by his family, his true love was his craft. Above all else he was dedicated to his art."[8]

Cook is acclaimed as one of the first cameramen to photograph the Civil War, and as one of the first to look upon the conflict as a photojournalist would (although that term wasn't known in Cook's time).

"History and the world owe much to the talent and initiative of Cook," said Thomas Peach, another of Cook's biographers. "Without his involvement, there would be no qualified Southern documentation of the Civil War at Fort Sumter and in Charleston."[9]

The Capital at War

At the time of the Civil War, Washington, D.C., did not look much like the city it is today. Its character was very different, too.

Many public buildings were unfinished. The Capitol itself lacked a dome, and work had stopped on the Washington Monument. In 1861 the monument was a mere stump, rising to less than a third of its ultimate height.

Gas lamps lighted the city's streets, all of which were unpaved, except for Pennsylvania Avenue. People got from one place to another mostly by walking. For long distances, they took a horse-drawn carriage or bus.

Sanitation was a major problem. The streets and vacant lots were strewn with garbage, and sewers from houses and hotels ran into open creeks, which flowed into the Potomac or Anacostia rivers.

Washington was a small city then, with a population of 61,122. Of that number, 9,209 were free black people and 1,744 were slaves.[1] (The Compromise of 1850 had abolished the trading of slaves in Washington, but it was still legal to own slaves there.)

Washington was a city of jangled nerves during the war. Virginia, a Confederate state, lay south and west of the city. Maryland, a border state, with much of the population loyal to the South, enclosed Washington to the north and east. Washingtonians were fearful that the city could be cut off from the rest of the Union. Once the war began, Lincoln was quick to send troops to Baltimore and other key locations in Maryland to help keep the state in the Union camp.

Washington was a divided city at the start of the war, home to many Southerners and Southern sympa-

At the time the Civil War began, many public buildings in Washington were unfinished. The Capitol itself lacked much of its dome. (Library of Congress)

Cows, sheep, pigs, and goats grazed in the area where the Washington Monument was under construction. In 1861 it was 154 feet in height. It rises to slightly more than 555 feet today. (National Archives)

thizers. They did not attempt to conceal their hatred for Union soldiers, often booing or hissing as columns of troops marched up Pennsylvania Avenue.

By mid-summer of 1861, the North and South had been at war for more than two months, yet no action of any importance had taken place. Many Northerners believed that one quick battle would bring an end to the conflict. The time had come to launch a strike.

In mid-July, Union General Irvin McDowell was ordered to lead an attack out of the capital into the central part of Virginia and capture Manassas Junction, some 25 miles from Washington. Manassas was important as a railroad junction.

While McDowell was a dedicated and experienced military leader, the approximately thirty thousand men he commanded were raw recruits who had rushed from states in the North to defend Washington. Lacking training and discipline, they were merely civilians who called themselves soldiers.[2]

As McDowell's force marched out toward Manassas, a Confederate army of about twenty thousand men, just as untried as the Union force, waited along the south bank of Bull Run, a slow-moving creek just north of Manassas.[3] The Confederates were under the command of General P. G. T. Beauregard, who had led the artillery attack on Fort Sumter.

McDowell struck on July 21, a hot Sunday, his troops hammering the left flank, or side, of the outmanned Southern line. At first, all went well for McDowell, and he telegraphed Washington that victory could be expected. But then Confederate reinforcements arrived on the battlefield, and the tide turned. McDowell, seeing that the attack had failed, called a retreat.

What began as an orderly withdrawal quickly turned into a rout. Hundreds of Washingtonians had journeyed out to see the battle, traveling in wagons and carriages of every description. Many had brought picnic lunches with them. When the thousands of soldiers and officers on foot, with their horse-drawn wagons, artillery pieces, and ambulances, swarmed toward the road leading to Washington and safety, they found their way blocked by a mass of civilians. Widespread panic was the result. The first battle of the Civil War was an embarrassment for the North.

Mathew Brady was at Bull Run that fateful Sunday in 1861, attempting to photograph the battle. Three years earlier, Brady had opened his Washington studio, managed by Alexander Gardner. The studio, on Pennsyl-

Union soldiers examine passenger credentials at the ferry landing at Mason's Island (now Theodore Roosevelt Memorial Island Park) across the Potomac River from Georgetown, which is a part of Washington today. George N. Barnard was the photographer. (Library of Congress)

vania Avenue between Sixth and Seventh Streets, had a sign that identified it as "Brady's National Photographic Art Gallery."

After the studio opened, Brady had returned to New York, leaving Gardner to supervise operations. But Brady was back in Washington early in 1861, perhaps to help arrange photographic coverage of Lincoln's inauguration and the first portrait photographs of the new president.

Brady was still in Washington at the time of Bull Run. Almost thirty years later, in an interview with the *New York World*, Brady was asked, "Did you have trouble getting to the war to take views?"

Brady replied: "I did have trouble; many objections were raised. However, I went to the first battle of Bull Run with two wagons from Washington. My personal companions were Dick McCormick, then a newspaper writer, Ned House; and Al Waud, the sketch artist.

"We stayed all night at Centreville; we got as far as Blackburne's Ford; we made pictures and expected to be in Richmond the next day, but it was not so and our apparatus was a good deal damaged on the way back to Washington."[4]

Timothy O'Sullivan, one of the photographers who worked for Brady at the time, also may have been at Bull Run. In an interview that appeared in *Harper's New Month-*ly Magazine in 1869, O'Sullivan said that "the Battle of Bull Run would have been photographed 'close-up' but for the fact that a shell from one of the Rebel field pieces took away the photographer's [O'Sullivan's] camera."[5]

All attempts at photographing the first important action of the Civil War apparently ended in failure, for no photographs of what is now referred to as the First Battle of Bull Run (or First Manassas, as the Southerners named the battle) have ever appeared.

Brady eventually did get photographs of Bull Run, in March 1862. By that time, the Confederates had given up the site for strategic reasons. George N. Barnard and James F. Gibson, two photographers from Brady's Washington studio, were assigned to visit Manassas and nearby towns and take photographs of Confederate fortifications and battlefield landmarks. Both Barnard and Gibson would later earn recognition as being among the Civil War's best cameramen.

The battle of Bull Run was an awakening. It made Northerners and the Federal government realize that the war was not going to be a short one.

In the months that followed, as Washington prepared for the long struggle that was to come, the city was transformed. The population would more than double during the war, mushrooming to almost 140,000.[6]

Harewood Hospital, one of Washington's largest, boasted land-scaped grounds and a flower garden. Here Harewood's surgeons pose for a photograph that is part of the Mathew Brady Collection at the National Archives. (National Archives)

Troops were everywhere. The Fifth Massachusetts Regiment was camped in the Treasury Building. (Each enlistee became part of a one-hundred-man company, often organized in a town or county. Ten companies, usually from the same state or area, were formed into a regiment.) The Eighth Massachusetts was quartered in the unfinished rotunda of the Capitol. Troops from Rhode Island lived near the Glenwood Cemetery.

The Lincoln administration, determined to make the capital safe from attack, constructed an extensive sys-

In downtown Washington at Armory Square, a huge public building was converted for use as a hospital. Streamers and flags decorate this ward at the Armory Square Hospital, perhaps indicating a holiday or even the war's end. (National Archives)

tem of fortifications. Twenty miles of trenches encircled the city. If the city should be threatened, the trenches would be occupied by armed soldiers.

Before the war's end in 1865, sixty-eight forts and artillery emplacements (called batteries), ringed the city. In addition, there were ninety-three smaller batteries equipped with field guns.[7]

As the war wore on and casualty lists got longer and longer, Washington was flooded with wounded from nearby battlefields. They arrived in two-wheeled or four-wheeled carts that served as ambulances. Special trains pulled boxcars loaded with wounded lying on thin mattresses or loose straw.

Washington had only one hospital at the beginning of the war, and that was soon overwhelmed. Public and private buildings were quickly taken over for hospital use. The Patent Office became the Patent Office Hospital. The Union Hotel in Georgetown, just west of the capital, became the Union Hotel Hospital. A barracks hospital was built on the south lawn of the White House, and after the battle of Gettysburg in 1863, hospital beds were put in the marble halls of the Capitol.

Scores of photographers were active in Washington during the war. Portrait photography was their mainstay. A steady stream of soldiers visited the studios of Mathew Brady and Alexander Gardner to have their portraits taken. Brady's cameramen made more than two hundred portrait photographs of the men from one regiment alone, the New York Seventh, headquartered at Camp Cameron in Washington.

Washington cameramen also documented forts and batteries, hospitals, and ambulance wagons. They took many scenic views of the city, as well.

After the war ended, Washington celebrated. On May 23 and 24, 1865, a Grand Review of the Federal Armies was staged up Washington's Pennsylvania Avenue. The streets were packed as Washingtonians paid final tribute to Northern soldiers and their commanding officers.

Brady's cameramen and Alexander Gardner were there to photograph the event. For a century and more, their images would be used to document what was the concluding event in a war that had tragically divided the city and the nation.

The Peninsular Campaign

During the Civil War, the mere mention of George B. McClellan's name was a sure way to start a debate or even a quarrel. Few were neutral about the young Union general.

To his supporters, McClellan, who was thirty-five when the war began, was devoted, enthusiastic, courageous, and intelligent. Early in the war, his brilliance as a military strategist and leader prompted newspapers to call him a "young Napoleon."

But to his opponents, the number of whom grew by leaps and bounds as the war progressed, McClellan was boastful and overly interested in furthering his personal ambitions. He enjoyed posing for the camera, and, in fact, ranks as one of the most photographed of all Civil War notables.

A graduate of West Point who had served in the Mexican War, in August 1861 McClellan was named by President Lincoln to command the Army of the Potomac. Using his talents as a leader and an organizer, McClellan molded what had been a scruffy, ragtag mass of recruits into the Union's main fighting force, described as "the best-equipped armed force ever assembled in the Western Hemisphere." With 150,000 men, the Army of the Potomac was also the biggest.[1]

From President Lincoln on down, the Union high command knew what they wanted to do with McClellan's massive army. Their focus was on Richmond. Not only was it the capital of the Confederacy, but Richmond was important as a transportation and manufacturing center. If the Confederacy lost Richmond, it would be a severe blow.

Some of the artillery and ammunition stockpiled by General McClellan on the Virginia peninsula for use during the Peninsular Campaign. This photograph was taken by one of Mathew Brady's cameramen after the fall of Yorktown. (Library of Congress)

Early in the spring of 1862, McClellan agreed to attempt to capture Richmond. But he did not plan to march directly south to the city, taking the overland route from Washington. McClellan's plan was to advance upon Richmond by water.

And that's exactly what he did, although Lincoln and several of his close advisors had no enthusiasm for the plan. They made McClellan leave a part of his army in Washington to defend the city in case of attack.

In mid-March, the Army of the Potomac was ready to move. A fleet of more than 450 vessels of every shape and size had been assembled. Carrying tens of thousands of Union soldiers, thousands of horses, hundreds of cannons, and tons of supplies, the ships eased away from wharves in Washington and Alexandria, Virginia, navigated down the Potomac River into Chesapeake Bay, and sailed south to Fort Monroe at the tip of the Virginia peninsula between the York and James rivers. It was one of the largest amphibious operations in the history of warfare up to that time.[2]

Once his men and their equipment were ashore, McClellan planned to advance north and east up the long, flat strip of land to Richmond, a distance of about 70 miles. Since the York and James rivers were controlled by the Union navy, its ships would be available with both supplies and firepower to support McClellan's campaign.

A Confederate army under the command of General Joseph E. Johnston waited for McClellan at Yorktown, which had been heavily fortified. But when McClellan prepared to shell the city with huge guns, Johnston's forces fell back to better defensive positions closer to Richmond. McClellan captured Yorktown without a fight.

As McClellan's army resumed its advance, the men and wagons were slowed more by unseasonable weather than by the Confederate army. During May it rained every day. The dirt roads became muck. Yet McClellan inched along, getting to within 10 miles of Richmond.

On the last day of May, Johnston ordered an advance upon a part of McClellan's army at the village of Seven Pines. During the fighting, Johnston was seriously wounded. To replace him, Confederate president Jefferson Davis chose General Robert E. Lee, a desk general at the time who had been serving as an advisor to Davis.

Lee's first move was to build up the fortifications in front of Richmond so that he would be able to defend the city with the fewest possible men. He sent out a call for General Thomas "Stonewall" Jackson and his hard-hitting army to join him at Richmond. Jackson had been

conducting a highly successful campaign in the Shenandoah Valley.

McClellan, meanwhile, was strengthening his battle line. He was being cautious because he believed—wrongly—that his Army of the Potomac was far outnumbered by the Confederate forces. He pleaded with Lincoln to send reinforcements.

The Peninsular Campaign reached a climax late in June when General Lee launched what became known as the Seven Days' Battles, which consisted of one violent flare-up after another—at Oak Grove, Mechanicsville, Gaine's Mill, Garnett's and Golding's Farms, Savage's Station and Allen's Farm, White Oak Hill, and, finally, Malvern Hill.

Lee didn't win every contest, but he managed to push McClellan's army back to the banks of the James River. In so doing, Lee saved Richmond.

McClellan blamed his defeat on lack of support from Washington. He refused to go on the offensive again until he received more men and supplies. Washington responded by ordering McClellan to give up the Peninsular Campaign and return north with the Army of the Potomac.

The Peninsular Campaign, which had begun in mid-March of 1862 and stretched deep into the summer, was

In the early stages of the Peninsular Campaign, huge mortars like these helped McClellan capture Yorktown with relative ease. Such guns could lob an iron cannonball, 13 inches in diameter—a basketball is 9 inches in diameter—and weighing more than 150 pounds, a distance of 2½ miles. (National Archives)

in easy reach of photographers based in Washington. It offered countless opportunities to cover battlefield action.

Photographers had been active earlier in the war, but their results had not been satisfactory. Brady himself had sought to photograph the First Battle of Bull Run, but in the frenzy of the Union retreat his camera and equipment had been wrecked.

Timothy O'Sullivan, who worked for Brady, had been particularly active during the first year of the war. Early in 1862, he traveled to South Carolina to photograph coastal bases captured by Union forces following a naval bombardment that had begun in November 1861. O'Sullivan had gotten photographs of camp scenes at Beaufort, South Carolina, artillery emplacements at Port Royal, and docks, sailors' graves, and a hospital camp at Hilton Head.

He had also photographed at Manassas early in 1862 after it had been abandoned by the Confederates. Brady photographers George N. Barnard and James F. Gibson had also photographed battlefield landmarks at Manassas.

But the Peninsular Campaign was different. It was not as frantic as Manassas had been during the fighting there. And it was not a site, such as Beaufort or Hilton

Head, where hostilities had ended. The Peninsular Campaign had live action but at a somewhat subdued pace.

Yorktown, the first objective of McClellan's campaign, was particularly attractive to the first photographers to arrive at Fort Monroe. Yorktown, after all, had been the scene of the last major battle of the American Revolution, where General George Washington and the Continental army surrounded the British army, forcing the surrender of British general Charles Cornwallis. That victory earned the United States its independence.

Gibson began work at Yorktown early in May, assisted by John Wood, who also worked at Brady's Washington studio.

Gibson's first photographs show McClellan's headquarters at Fort Winfield Scott, near Yorktown. He also took scenic views of Yorktown.

Civil War cameramen spent a good part of their time taking pictures of Union officers and their staff members. This group, photographed during the Peninsular Campaign before the fighting started, includes (in the foreground at the right with the dog) George A. Custer, a twenty-two-year-old captain and member of McClellan's staff. A major general at the war's end, Custer was later engaged in Indian fighting. He died along with the men under his command at the battle of Little Big Horn in June 1876. (Library of Congress)

Several of the Yorktown photographs stress the town's connection to the American Revolution. One photograph is captioned "Headquarters of Lord Cornwallis...now used as a Hospital, under the Superintendence of Miss Dix." (Dorothea Dix was superintendent of Union nurses during the Civil War.) Other photographs showed the headquarters of the Marquis de Lafayette, the French soldier and statesman who played a major role in Washington's victory.

Once the Southern army had abandoned Yorktown to McClellan's army, Gibson and the other photographers switched their attention to the elaborate fortifications that had been built by the Confederates. They also took a great number of photographs of artillery units and group portraits of generals and members of their staffs.

Gibson accompanied the Army of the Potomac in its drive toward Richmond—with splendid results. His panoramic view of the vast number of Union soldiers camped at Cumberland Landing on the Pamunkey River revealed the massive nature of the campaign. Of all the war photographs taken up to that time, none was so dramatic.

During the final stages of the Peninsular Campaign, when Lee attacked McClellan's army in the Seven Days' Battles, Gibson was at Savage's Station, one of the battle sites. There he photographed wounded Union soldiers awaiting treatment. These images still stir deep feelings.

❧ ❧❧ ❧

Little is known of James F. Gibson. As a photographer, he was obviously greatly skilled. He also had the courage, determination, and energy required to accompany an army into battle.

Like Alexander Gardner, Gibson was born in Scotland. He was in his early thirties when the Civil War began, and working in Mathew Brady's Washington studio, which was being managed by Gardner.[3]

After the Peninsular Campaign, Gibson continued to distinguish himself. In September 1862, he and Gardner and O'Sullivan photographed at Antietam (Chapter 5), and he was with Gardner at Gettysburg (Chapter 7). Gibson photographed at Falmouth, Fredericksburg, Brandy Station, and other sites in Virginia during 1863 and 1864.

During the Peninsular Campaign, James F. Gibson, working for Mathew Brady at the time, captured this remarkable sweeping view of a portion of McClellan's Army of the Potomac camped at Cumberland Landing on the Pamunkey River. (Library of Congress)

A field hospital at Savage's Station, Virginia, where one of the Seven Days' Battles was staged, as photographed by James F. Gibson late in June 1862. The sick and wounded lie on the ground waiting treatment. (Library of Congress)

In 1864, Gibson took over the management of Brady's Washington studio, which was having serious financial problems. However, he lacked business ability and was unable to make the studio profitable. He and Brady quarreled and ended up suing each other. Gibson left Washington for Kansas in 1868.[4]

It is for the vivid and timely photographs that he produced during the Peninsular Campaign that Gibson is remembered. To other cameramen of the time, they served as an example of what to expect in a war zone, the photographic opportunities, and what it was possible to achieve.

CHAPTER

Antietam

Late in September 1862, from the village of Sharpsburg in western Maryland, an officer from Wisconsin wrote to his brother: "We were in a fearful battle at this place on the 17th—it was a great enormous battle—a great tumbling of all heaven and earth. The slaughter on both sides was enormous."[1]

The Wisconsin officer did not exaggerate. On September 17, 1862, the two main armies of the Civil War met in combat along the banks of a slow-moving stream known as Antietam Creek, about three-quarters of a mile east of Sharpsburg. After that one day of fighting, some four thousand men lay dead, and more than twenty-one thousand others were missing or wounded.[2]

The battle of Antietam was the bloodiest day of the Civil War, the bloodiest day in American history, in fact.[3]

General Lee and his Confederate forces were filled with optimism in the days before Antietam. Late in August 1862, the Confederates had pinned a major defeat on the Union army at a battle known as the Second Battle of Bull Run (or Second Manassas), just 25 miles from Washington. The capital was in a state of great anxiety.

While the battered Union army fretted about its blunders at Manassas, Lee moved boldly. It was time, he believed, to invade the North. He set forth a plan calling for his Confederate army to march north out of Virginia into Maryland and, with success there, perhaps into Pennsylvania as well.

Lee hoped that by moving into Maryland he might induce the people of that border state to join the Confederacy, thus surrounding Washington by enemy territory.

Equally important, Lee and other Confederate leaders felt that a decisive victory in the North might cause Great Britain and France to recognize the Confederacy as an independent nation and perhaps even to enter the war on their side.

During the first week in September, Lee's army of some fifty thousand men crossed the Potomac River into Maryland at White's Ford, 25 miles northwest of Wash-

Signal stations played an important role during the fighting at Antietam Creek. In a caption he wrote in his Photographic Sketch Book of the War, *published in 1866, Gardner declared: "At intervals along our line of battle, and on the most prominent points in the vicinity, were stationed the Federal signal officers, detecting by their skill, vigilance, and powerful glasses, every movement of the enemy, reporting them by a few waves of the flag to the Union Commander." On Elk Ridge (or Elk Mountain), about 2½ miles east of Sharpsburg, the Federal signal corps constructed this signal station of crisscrossed logs that provided panoramic views of the battlefield and the village of Sharpsburg itself.* (Library of Congress)

ington, and then marched toward the town of Frederick.[4] Once there, Lee divided his army. He ordered General James Longstreet and three divisions north to capture Hagerstown, and sent General Stonewall Jackson and six divisions to seize Harpers Ferry, where the Shenandoah River joined the Potomac. Once he controlled Harpers Ferry, Lee could bring the supplies his army needed through the protected Shenandoah Valley.

Meanwhile, a Federal army of more than eighty-five thousand men under the command of General McClellan had marched out of Washington in pursuit of Lee. McClellan, fearing that Lee might be setting a trap, moved cautiously. By the time McClellan's army reached Frederick, Lee was gone.[5]

Stonewall Jackson's efforts to capture Harpers Ferry took longer than expected because of stiff Federal resistance. Lee was moving through Sharpsburg when he received the news of Jackson's victory.

Lee was well aware that he was being pursued by McClellan, and he fully realized that should he be attacked, he was in danger of defeat because his forces were split. So Lee decided to remain in Sharpsburg and there gather his divisions together.

Sharpsburg, about 10 miles north of Harpers Ferry, was a good location to defend. The ground just west of the creek offered a slight rise along the Hagerstown Pike that held a commanding view of the creek, its bridges, and the shallow places where it could be crossed on foot. With only nineteen thousand men available, and facing an enemy that was three or four times as strong, Lee needed every advantage he could get.

McClellan's men began trickling up to Antietam Creek on September 15. "Little Mac," as McClellan was sometimes called, spent much of that day and all of the next planning the battle and getting his units properly placed. Lee waited.

The next day, fighting began at dawn and did not stop for fourteen hours. McClellan never used his superior numbers for a concentrated assault upon the Confederate positions. Instead, he attacked piecemeal, first at daybreak, then at noon, and, finally, during the afternoon.

Lee managed to fend off the attacks by skillfully shifting men from one site to another. There was fierce fighting at several places now well known to Civil War historians: Dunker Church, the East Woods, the West Woods, Bloody Lane, and the Corn Field.

Some of the most desperate fighting during the battle of Antietam occurred at Burnside Bridge. Confederate forces defended the bridge from the creek's steep banks, pouring rifle and artillery fire down upon Union soldiers. This view, taken by either Gardner or Gibson after the battle, shows some of the damage that the bridge sustained. The Burnside Bridge still stands, operated as part of a national battlefield under the direction of the National Park Service. (Library of Congress)

Burnside Bridge is another name that has become legendary. (At the time, it was known as Rohrbach Bridge because it was near the town of Rohrbach.) After several hours of fighting, McClellan ordered General Ambrose Burnside's Ninth Corps to storm over the bridge and attack Lee's forces on the other side. On their first attempt, Burnside's men were pinned down by the entrenched Confederates and got only as far as the bridge approaches. When the Northern army tried a second time, they made it to the bridge but were thrown back by heavy Confederate rifle and artillery fire.

The Confederates had been firing for three hours and were running low on ammunition when the Federals launched their third attempt. This time, Burnside's men forced their way across the bridge that has since carried the general's name.

Once on the other side, the Federals, despite heavy losses, regrouped and struck out for Sharpsburg. At this critical moment, a Confederate division of three thousand men under the command of General A. P. Hill arrived from Harpers Ferry after a seven-hour march. Without resting, Hill's men attacked Burnside's left flank, which crumbled. By sundown, Burnside's troops had been pushed back to the bridge once more.

McClellan felt that his army was too crippled to continue the assault the next day. As for Lee, his generals convinced him that a counterattack was impossible. On the night of September 18, Lee crossed back over the Potomac into Virginia, saddened by the great number of casualties his army had suffered and the realization that his invasion of the North had failed.

Although the battle of Antietam cannot be considered a victory for the North, at least it was not another in the Union's string of woeful defeats. Lincoln used this turn of fortune to announce his Emancipation Proclamation, which granted freedom to all slaves in Confederate states.

At about the same time that General Lee retreated across the Potomac River with his grieving army, Alexander Gardner arrived at the Antietam battlefield from Washington. Gardner was accompanied by James F. Gibson, who already ranked as one of the war's most skilled and experienced photographers. Earlier in 1862, Gibson had covered General McClellan's unsuccessful Peninsular Campaign, producing some of the most striking war photographs yet to be seen. Gardner and Gibson were employed by Mathew Brady at the time.

Gardner's Antietam photographs were to create a sensation. And no wonder. No other American battlefield had been photographed so soon after the fighting.[6] As a result, Gardner was able to document the horror of a battlefield spread with the bodies of dead soldiers. Gardner recorded both Confederate and Union dead—

In a catalog he prepared of his Civil War images, Gardner titled this photograph: "Dead: Horse of a Confederate Colonel; both killed at the Battle of Antietam." The horse belonged to Colonel Henry B. Strong from Louisiana. His body was recovered by his men and buried near Dunker Church. Because the horse had such a lifelike appearance, battlefield observers had a difficult time believing that the animal was actually dead. (Library of Congress)

Gardner's photos of the battlefield dead at Antietam stunned people of the day. This view depicts the bodies of Confederate soldiers, members of General William E. Starke's Louisiana brigade, photographed where they fell along the Hagerstown Pike. (Library of Congress)

near Dunker Church, along the Hagerstown Pike, in the Bloody Lane, and near the Miller barn.

Some seventy photographs were taken within five days of the battle—sixty-three by Gardner, seven by Gibson.[7] Presumably, Gibson spent most of his time preparing and developing the glass plates used by Gardner.

Late in October that year, the public got to see many of these photographs through an exhibition staged by Mathew Brady at his celebrated studio in New York City. Titled "The Dead at Antietam," the photographs showed dead Americans lying stiff, their arms outstretched, their

The village of Sharpsburg, located about a three-quarters of a mile west of Antietam Creek, was transformed by the fighting. Only a few structures survived without damage from the intense Union artillery fire. Almost every building left standing was turned into a hospital, including Saint Paul's Episcopal Church, which appears to the left of center in the background of this view of the village taken by Gardner. (Library of Congress)

bodies swollen, along country roads and in empty cornfields. People were stunned by what they saw.

Said the *New York Times*: "The dead of the battlefield come up to us very rarely, even in dreams. We see lists in the morning paper at breakfast, but dismiss its recollection with the coffee. Mr. Mathew Brady has done something to bring home to us the terrible reality and earnestness of the war. If he has not brought bodies and laid them in our dooryards and along our streets, he has done something very like it."[8]

Several of Gardner's Antietam photographs were also copied for use as engravings by *Harper's Weekly*. The photographs were taken, the magazine declared, "by the well known and enterprising photographer, Mr. M. B. Brady."[9] It must have upset Gardner to see someone else receive credit for what were being hailed as the most startling battlefield photographs ever produced.

During the first week in October, Abraham Lincoln visited Antietam to meet with General McClellan. The president wanted to find out why McClellan had not pursued General Lee's army as it retreated into Virginia. (Several weeks after the meeting, Lincoln relieved McClellan of his command, replacing him with General Burnside.)

Early in October 1862, about two weeks after the battle, President Lincoln visited Sharpsburg and the Antietam battlefield to meet with General McClellan. While there, he posed with McClellan for this Gardner photograph, one of the most famous Civil War images. According to Gardner's Sketch Book, when the president complained to McClellan about his failure to pursue General Lee as he retreated into Virginia, the general is said to have replied, "You will find those who will go faster than I, Mr. President; but it is very doubtful if you will find many who will go further." (Library of Congress)

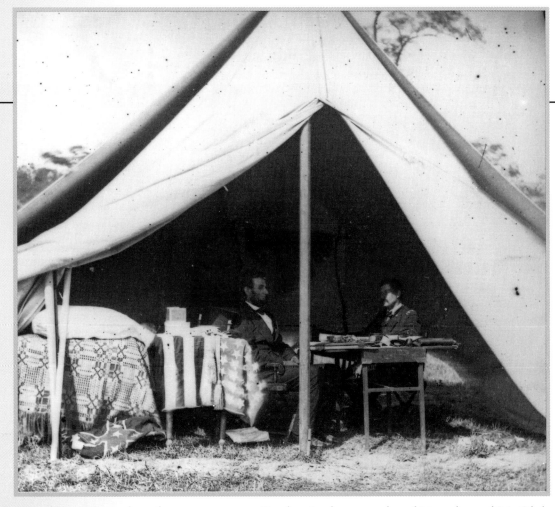

Gardner was there during Lincoln's visit and took several photographs of the president and General McClellan and members of McClellan's staff. While Lincoln met with his generals in the field on a number of occasions, this was his only visit that was documented by a camera. Gardner's photographs of Lincoln and McClellan are among the most famous of all Civil War images. But it is for his shocking views of the battlefield dead at Antietam that Alexander Gardner is best remembered.

Soldier Portraits

Mathew Brady, Alexander Gardner, James F. Gibson, and Timothy O'Sullivan, plus several others, are the names normally identified with Civil War photography. But their work represents only a small part of the picture-taking that was done during the war. Most of the many thousands of Civil War photographers specialized in portrait photography—likenesses of enlisted men and officers.

Not only did every city and town have portrait studios, but some photographers set up temporary facilities at sites where large numbers of soldiers were encamped. Usually these portraits were sent home to family and friends.

"So many soldiers' portraits were taken that early in the war the postal system ground to a halt because of the number and weight of photographic likenesses being sent through the mail," notes William Stapp, former curator of photography at the Smithsonian Institution's National Portrait Gallery, in *Landscapes of the Civil War*.[1]

Big-city studios were often quite elaborate. At Mathew Brady's studio on Pennsylvania Avenue in Washington, operations were spread over several floors. The first floor was a reception area decorated with enlargements of Brady portraits to occupy customers while they waited. The second floor was where the finishing and mounting rooms were located.

On the top floor, the camera operator and his assistants posed their subjects.[2] Strewn about the floor were cameras, camera stands, painted backdrops, posing chairs, and props used in the photographs, such as tables, drapes,

Soldiers of a New York regiment pose for the camera against a plain backdrop at Mathew Brady's studio in New York. Skylights in the ceiling and at one side provided illumination. (National Archives)

Private Benjamin B. Hart of New York, an infantryman, posed for this carte-de-visite *portrait with a pistol and binoculars, which are likely to have been props furnished by the photographer. Private Hart died in November 1862 of wounds that he had suffered at the Second Battle of Bull Run.* (Collection of Thomas Harris)

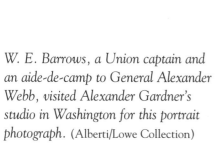

W. E. Barrows, a Union captain and an aide-de-camp to General Alexander Webb, visited Alexander Gardner's studio in Washington for this portrait photograph. (Alberti/Lowe Collection)

A painted backdrop depicting an army campground was used to enhance this portrait of a Union officer, believed to be Captain George Hunt of the Twelfth Regiment, Illinois Volunteer Infantry. (Collection of Thomas Harris)

or tall columns. For soldier photographs, the props might include swords, caps, field glasses, and a rifle or pistol.

When Brady opened his studio in Washington, he added a skylight to admit the sunlight required to make the exposure. Skylights were a standard feature in most studios of the day. Curtains, mirrors, and screens were used to control the amount of light that poured in.

The subject usually sat in a straight-back posing chair. Opposite the chair was the camera, mounted on a tripod, or wooden stand. The camera was fitted with a brass tube at the front that held the lens.

In some studios, there was a painted curtain behind the subject. For soldier portraits, this backdrop often depicted an outdoor scene that featured cannons, tents, flags, or other battlefield objects.

Just before the picture was taken, a metal clamp was fastened to the back of the subject's head or neck. The clamp was fixed to a long metal rod that was anchored in a heavy metal base. This device kept the subject's head perfectly still during the time of the exposure, which usually lasted from five to ten seconds. The tiniest movement could cause a blur.

When all was ready, the photographer viewed the scene on a special glass plate at the back of the camera. He draped a black cloth over his head and the back of the camera to shut out the light and make the image on the glass easier to see. As he viewed the subject through the lens, he carefully focused.

Then the focusing glass was removed from the camera and the sensitized glass negative was inserted in its place. A thin metal slide was removed so the negative could be exposed.[3]

The cameraman then may have chatted briefly with the subject, seeking to get a relaxed expression. At the right instant, the cameraman removed the cap that covered the camera lens.

"Don't move!" the cameraman would say. "Don't even breathe!"

When the cameraman judged enough light had entered the lens to expose the glass plate, the cap was placed back over the lens.

While the customer waited, the glass plate was developed and prints made. It usually took about an hour. The prints, called *cartes de visite*, were relatively small in size, measuring 2½ by 4 inches, and had a brownish, or sepia, tone. A dozen cost about $2.50 to $3.[4]

Cartes de visite had been introduced in America from France in 1859. Within a year, they had become wildly popular.

This tintype of a young soldier, wearing a Hardee hat and holding a rifle and saber bayonet, dates from 1861 or 1862. The photograph, probably a gift to a loved one, was placed in a handsome case behind a decorated brass mat and protective glass. (Collection of Thomas Harris)

Photographer Sam A. Cooley, who made this portrait of a young Union officer, operated several studios in South Carolina and one in Jacksonville, Florida. He also made views in South Carolina during the time that Confederate forces held the state. Later, Cooley was assigned as a photographer to the Union's Tenth Army Corps. (Alberti/Lowe Collection)

Not only were family portraits produced in *carte-de-visite* form, but the pictures of notables of the day were also available. CDVs, as they are often called, could be purchased with the images of President Lincoln, Queen Victoria and other foreign leaders, Civil War generals, prominent women, statesmen, clergymen, and actors and actresses. Few homes were without a CDV album in which the small pictures were mounted.

Alexander Gardner was among the first to perceive the profit to be made from publishing such photographs. Gardner ordered a special four-lens camera that was capable of making multiple exposures of each pose. He thus quadrupled the number of prints that could be derived from just one exposure.

In 1856 another type of photographic process was introduced. The subject's image was captured on a small metal plate that was exposed in the camera. It was known as the tintype, although the plate actually was made of sheet iron, not tin.

Among Civil War soldiers, tintypes became even more popular than *cartes de visite*. The metal plate was much more durable than the small rectangle of thin cardboard and thus could be sent through the mail with much less risk of being damaged.

Also, the tintype was cheap, a fact that appealed to the poorly paid Civil War enlisted man. Once cameras were available that could make multiple exposures on one plate, tintypes were sold for as little as four for 25¢.[5]

The tintype portrait was usually inserted in a paper sleeve that had an oval cutout to frame the image. Or it could be placed in a small wooden or plastic case in which the image was framed by a sheet-brass mat and protected with glass.

Tintypes remained popular throughout the war among both Northern and Southern soldiers. In the South, however, their use declined as the war continued because of a shortage of iron in sheet form.

Tintypes and *cartes de visite* are still with us. They were produced in such an enormous quantity that they're often available for purchase at flea markets or antique shows. Usually they cost no more than a dollar or two. Soldier portraits in these formats are scarce, however, having been snapped up by collectors, although occasionally it's possible to make a valuable find.

Gettysburg

In the spring of 1863, General Robert E. Lee was filled with optimism. His confidence sprang from victories by his Army of Northern Virginia, first at Fredericksburg, Virginia, in December 1862, and then, in May 1863, at Chancellorsville, also in Virginia.

Lee decided that it was once again time to take the initiative, to go on the attack, and seek a victory on Northern soil. The Confederate leader held the lingering hope that a decisive battlefield victory in the North would bring help from foreign sources and might even get the Union to the peace table.

On June 3, 1863, Lee's army of seventy-five thousand Confederates marched out of Maryland into southern Pennsylvania, then headed eastward.[1] On the out-

skirts of the little town of Gettysburg, where a number of important roads converged, the Confederates clashed with Northern cavalrymen, the advance elements of the Army of Potomac, now under the command of the hot-tempered but reliable General George G. Meade. What was a chance encounter on June 30 would quickly intensify to become one of the most significant battles of the war, often cited as its turning point.

The battle at Gettysburg lasted three days. Fighting began on the morning of July 1 just west of town and continued through the day. The Northern forces were badly outnumbered at first, since only a portion of their army had arrived, and they fell back to the ridges south of Gettysburg. The town itself was occupied by Southern troops.

Over the next two days, Lee attacked the Union

right and left flanks repeatedly. But the Northerners, now reinforced, held their positions.

As July 3 dawned, Lee was faced with a decision. He could either make an all-out assault against the center of the Northern line or call a retreat.

Lee acted with characteristic boldness. He ordered 13,500 men under General George E. Pickett to advance almost a mile across open ground toward the central Union position on Cemetery Ridge.[2] "Pickett's charge," as the assault was called, resulted in terrible carnage.

As soon as the advancing Confederate soldiers came within range, they were raked with shelling from Union cannons. Yet the men pushed on, absorbing fire from Northern infantrymen posted behind stone walls and hastily built mounds of earth. Broken by their enormous losses, Pickett's men fell back to their lines. The battle of Gettysburg was over, a jolting loss for General Lee.

Meade's Army of the Potomac suffered twenty-three thousand casualties, including 3,100 killed. The Confederates had lost nearly as many. For the two armies, the dead numbered more than six thousand.[3]

The next day, July 4, both armies were too exhausted to do much else than recover their wounded from the field and start burying their dead. Toward the end of the day, a deeply saddened General Lee marched his men back toward the Potomac River and Southern soil. The Army of Northern Virginia would not attempt to invade the North again.

❧ ❧ ❧

On July 3, two days after the fighting had begun, the first reports of the battle were received in Washington. Alexander Gardner, Timothy O'Sullivan and James F. Gibson were the first photographers to react to the news.

By this time, O'Sullivan and Gibson worked for Alexander Gardner, not Mathew Brady. Gardner had split with Brady late in 1862 and opened his own studio in Washington. One of Gardner's first moves was to hire several cameramen who had worked in the field for Brady. These included O'Sullivan, Gibson, and Gardner's own brother James.

At the time they received the first battle reports from Gettysburg, Gardner, O'Sullivan, and Gibson apparently already had their wagons loaded and were ready to move, for the three men arrived in Gettysburg, which lay 77 miles northwest of Washington, on Sunday, July 5. Once on the battlefield, they immediately set up their equipment and began making photographs.

Gardner had a personal interest in events at Gettysburg: His fifteen-year-old son, Lawrence, was a student at a boarding school in Emmitsburg, Maryland, only 10

Alexander Gardner originally titled this photograph "A Harvest of Death." Taken by Timothy O'Sullivan, it pictures Union dead gathered for burial at Gettysburg. (Library of Congress)

miles south of the battle site. Gardner is believed to have stopped at the school to visit his son and make sure that he was unharmed.

Gardner, O'Sullivan, and Gibson reached Gettysburg by way of the Emmitsburg Road not long before noon on July 5. The southern portion of the battlefield near the Rose woods and farm was still strewn with bodies. Operating as a team, Gardner and his colleagues went to work, making about twenty images, mostly of battlefield dead.[4]

Gardner is likely to have gone to Gettysburg with the idea of concentrating on subjects that would testify to the war's horrors. From the series of photographs he had taken at Antietam almost two years earlier, Gardner knew that such images evoked the strongest emotional response from the press and public. He also realized that

This panoramic view of Gettysburg was made by Timothy O'Sullivan on July 7, 1863, just a few days after the battle had ended. The campground of a Northern militia unit appears in the foreground at the right.
(Library of Congress)

they had the greatest commercial appeal. Of the approximately sixty photographs that Gardner and his associates took at Gettysburg, about forty depict battlefield dead, or open graves, or otherwise document the slaughter that took place.

On Monday, July 6, their second day at Gettysburg, Gardner, O'Sullivan, and Gibson focused their attention on the aftermath of the fighting, which had engulfed a

number of dramatic rock formations known as Devil's Den. Most of their photographs were taken that day.

On Tuesday, July 7, their final day at the battlefield, the three cameramen moved closer to the town itself. O'Sullivan produced a splendid scenic view of the town, with a mass of soldiers' tents in the foreground. Another O'Sullivan photograph pictures a battered barn, its yard littered with dead horses.

Because Gardner and his associates were the first cameramen to arrive at Gettysburg, they were able to record scenes that would be available to no other photographers. The images they recorded capture the true horror of the battle.

A week or ten days after Gardner, O'Sullivan, and Gibson had left Gettysburg for Washington, Mathew Brady arrived at the battlefield, with two or three assistants. By that time, the dead had been buried and other gruesome aspects of the fighting had been wiped away.

Brady therefore took a different approach. His photographers, who recorded only about thirty images, concentrated on the landmarks of the battle and subjects of historical significance. They photographed Lee's headquarters, the Lutheran Seminary, Pennsylvania College, the gateway to Gettysburg Cemetery, a rocky hill named Little Round Top, which figured importantly in the fighting, and John Burns, a resident of Gettysburg and a veteran of the War of 1812, who fought on the Union side during the battle. They also took several panoramic views of the battlefield and the surrounding community.[5]

Brady and his cameramen seemed to have worked at a more leisurely pace, for many of their images are notable for their sharp focus and richness in detail.

Harper's Weekly, in its issue of August 22, 1863, featured Brady's work at Gettysburg. Several engravings based on Brady's photographs appeared in the magazine. Each carried a credit line that read: "Photograph by Brady."

The publication hailed Brady as the photographer "to whose industry and energy we are indebted for many of the most reliable war pictures."[6] Alexander Gardner's work had again been overshadowed by Brady and his reputation.

The Brady and Gardner teams were not the only cameramen to photograph at Gettysburg. The Tyson brothers, Charles and Isaac, owners of a photographic

Civil War photographs were not always truthful in what they pictured. This image, titled "Home of a Rebel Sharpshooter," taken by Gardner, is a case in point. O'Sullivan and Gardner originally photographed this young man's body at a different location, then moved it to the rock formation pictured here because of its visual appeal. They also propped a rifle against the rock wall (although it was not the type of rifle used by Confederate sharpshooters). The image is one of the most famous of all Gettysburg photographs. (National Archives)

studio in Gettysburg, also made photographs of battlefield sites in August 1863. And Frederick Gutekunst, a well-known Philadelphia photographer, took several battlefield views, as well.[7]

Shortly after the Civil War, Gardner selected one hundred images from the nearly three thousand photographs that he and his associates had taken and published them in *Gardner's Photographic Sketch Book of the War.* Lengthy captions explained each photograph.

Originally published as a two-volume work, the *Sketch Book* cost $150, a sizable amount for that time. Gardner planned to publish 200 copies.

About fifty copies of the *Sketch Book* are known to exist today. The work is breathtaking to see in its original

Mathew Brady and his team of assistants spent two or three days at Gettysburg and made approximately thirty photographs there. They include this picture of Brady himself, a photograph that Brady titled "Wheatfield in which General Reynolds was Shot." (National Archives)

form. All of the photographs have been "tipped in," that is, an original print of each of the one hundred has been pasted to an album page. Gardner's commentary for each photograph occupies a facing page. Of the thousands of books published about the Civil War, this is one of the most effective in conveying the tragic nature and emotional power of the conflict.

"The publication of the *Sketch Book* climaxed Alexander Gardner's contribution to Civil War photography and his career as a photographer," says William Stapp of the National Portrait Gallery. "It remains an incredibly powerful work today, and that is a testament to the genius and craft of Alexander Gardner, its creator."[8]

To Atlanta and the Sea

Early in March 1864, President Lincoln promoted Ulysses S. Grant to the rank of lieutenant general and gave him command of all the Union armies. A no-nonsense, straightforward, and very determined military leader, Grant wasted no time in devising a two-pronged plan to win the war.

Grant's strategy called for the Army of the Potomac to move toward Richmond, seeking not so much to capture the city as to confront and destroy the Army of Northern Virginia led by General Robert E. Lee.

At the same time, Grant ordered General William T. Sherman, who was in charge of the western theater of operations, to push south and east from Tennessee into Georgia and capture the city of Atlanta, a supply, manu-

facturing, and communications center that was vital to the South.

Grant's instructions were very precise. He told Sherman: "to move against [General Joseph E.] Johnston's army, to break it up, and to get into the interior of the enemy's country as far as you can, inflicting all the damage you can against their war resources."[1]

Sherman achieved these goals—and much more.

His campaign began in May 1864 in Chatanooga, Tennessee, included the "March to the Sea" from Atlanta to Savannah, Georgia, during the fall of 1864, and drew to a close near Durham, North Carolina, in April 1865.[2]

During the long trek, Sherman and his army were accompanied by veteran photographer George N.

General William T. Sherman, Grant's best general, had uncombed hair, a reddish beard, a frown, and, often, a wild expression in his eyes. (National Archives)

Barnard. Talented and exacting, the forty-five-year-old Barnard had been active as a war photographer since 1861 and the First Battle of Bull Run. Barnard had been named the official photographer of the Military Division of Mississippi, which was commanded by General Sherman, in 1862.

Sherman's bold march to Atlanta and beyond, together with Grant's operations against Lee at Petersburg and Richmond, helped to bring the Civil War to an end. Barnard covered the Sherman campaign from start to finish. He photographed Sherman and his generals, Confederate and Union fortifications, important battle sites, and the destruction wrought by Sherman's marauding soldiers, providing the only visual record of one of the war's most devastating and decisive military operations.

In confronting Sherman's army, General Johnston used hit-and-run tactics to avoid risking an all-out battle in the field. His army would make brief stands, then fall back.

Sherman made steady progress. By the middle of July, his army had crossed the Chattahoochee River and reached the edge of Atlanta. Johnston's army occupied the earthen embankments that surrounded the city.

Many Southerners, including Jefferson Davis, president of the Confederacy, were disappointed by Johnston's defensive tactics. Davis replaced Johnston with General John B. Hood, younger and bolder than Johnston.

Hood moved quickly to attack. But Hood's forays were beaten back by Sherman, with the Confederates suffering heavy losses.

The Atlanta railroad station not long after the city was occupied by Sherman's army. A line of army supply wagons is pictured at the left. Sherman ordered all civilians out of the city, then blew up the banks and destroyed the railroad station. (Library of Congress)

Sherman then began shifting his forces, maneuvering to encircle the city and to cut the rail lines that carried supplies to the Confederates. When Hood realized that he could not hold the city, he retreated south. Sherman's army occupied Atlanta on September 2, 1864.

Sherman paused in Atlanta for two months, resting his soldiers and stockpiling supplies. He ordered all civilians out of the city. Many of their abandoned homes were looted or burned, or both.

On November 15, Sherman launched what was to become his most famous military operation, marching his men to Savannah and the sea, 285 miles to the south and east. They encountered little resistance and moved at a leisurely pace. To the soldiers, says historian Bruce Catton, it was "more like a prolonged picnic than like regular war."[3]

As the army advanced, Sherman's soldiers plundered and destroyed almost everything in their path. Sherman did not try to stop them. Savannah fell to Sherman in December 1864.

After Savannah, Sherman turned north. In mid-February 1865, Sherman's army occupied Columbia, South Carolina. The city was set ablaze. Charleston and Fort Sumter were the next to fall.

Sherman's soldiers kept moving north through South Carolina, looting and destroying, and into North Carolina. General Johnston, who had been sent to North Carolina after being replaced by Hood, told Lee: "Sherman's force cannot be hindered by the small force I have. I can do no more than annoy him."[4]

But Lee's own situation as he faced Grant at Petersburg was even more desperate. There could be no doubt now: The Confederacy was doomed.

George N. Barnard was already highly skilled and experienced as a photographer when he joined General Sherman in the spring of 1864. Born in Coventry, Connecticut, on December 23, 1819, George was given the middle name Norman in honor of his father, who died when George was six years old. After his father's death, the family moved to central New York state.

Barnard married in 1843 at the age of 24. He and his wife settled in Oswego, New York, where Barnard helped to manage a hotel. By this time, Barnard had become interested in photography. In 1846 he gave up the hotel business to open a daguerreotype studio in Oswego.[5] He quickly became well known for his fine portrait work.

On the night of July 5, 1853, a great fire engulfed a good part of the city of Oswego. According to the Syra-

The fire that raged through Columbia, South Carolina, destroyed or damaged several churchs, dozens of private homes, and many public buildings. The state house itself did not escape— as this Barnard photograph shows. (National Archives)

On February 17, 1865, Sherman's army occupied Columbia, South Carolina, the state's capital. A fire broke out that wrought enormous damage. This Barnard photograph shows the widespread devastation. (National Archives)

George N. Barnard, one of the most skilled and admired of all Civil War photographers. (Alberti/Lowe Collection)

cuse *Daily Standard*, the blaze spread "with astonishing rapidity," until a large section of the city was reduced to "a mass of ashes."[6]

Barnard was there with his daguerreotype camera to document the disaster. He made at least two views of the blaze, which historians now cite as being among the earliest news photographs ever taken in America. One shows a grain storage building completely wrapped in flames. Beside it is a similar structure, its upper floors all but swallowed up in smoke.

Barnard fully understood the commercial value of the photographs that he took that night. He made copies of the daguerreotypes and advertised their availability in local newspapers for several months after the fire.

"If by the 1860s, he [Barnard] was not known as a photojournalist," says Michael L. Carlebach in *The Origins of Photojournalism in America*, "it is because the word had not yet been invented."[7]

By 1861, and the outbreak of the Civil War, Barnard had become a member of Mathew Brady's team of pho-

tographers in Washington, D.C. In July of that year, Barnard was assigned to cover the First Battle of Bull Run. No photographs of that battle, a stunning defeat for the Northern forces, have ever come to light. Barnard, like Mathew Brady and hundreds of spectators, got caught up in the Northerners' panicky retreat.

According to an article that appeared in *Anthony's Photographic Bulletin* in 1902, as Barnard attempted to return to Washington following the fighting at Bull Run, he "overtook a poor fellow, sorely wounded in the leg, trying to get back to Washington." Barnard gave up his space in his wagon to the man, the article said, then "shouldered his heavy instrument, and, after weary walking, he reached Washington, footsore and tired."[8]

Early in 1862, Barnard, along with James F. Gibson, returned to Bull Run to photograph the battle's landmarks. Eight of his images were later published by Gardner in the first volume of his *Photographic Sketch Book of the War.*

Barnard returned to Oswego later in 1862 for a short stay. In September, a photography studio in Oswego proclaimed in a local newspaper that it had "secured the services for a limited time of that celebrated artist George N. Barnard (formerly of this city, and of late from Brady's Gallery, Washington.)"[9]

Barnard resumed his role as a war photographer in 1864, joining Sherman's army as it marched from Tennessee through Georgia, then north into the Carolinas. His images, many of which capture the grim reality of the campaign's destructiveness, helped to establish Barnard as one of the standout documentary photographers of the time.

After the war, Barnard gathered sixty-one of these photographs and had them published in book form. To explain the images, he published a separate booklet with maps.

Titled *Photographic Views of Sherman's Campaign*, the book was highly praised by *Harper's Weekly* in its issue of December 8, 1866. Said *Harper's*: "These photographs are views of important places, of noted battlefields, of military works; and, for the care and judgment in selecting the point of view, for the delicacy of execution, for scope of treatment, and for the fidelity of impression, they surpass any other photographic views which have been pro-duced in this country."[10] Several photographs from that book are reproduced in this chapter.

Barnard later operated photography studios in Chicago and Charleston, South Carolina. He photographed the devastation of the great Chicago fire in 1871. Barnard's operation in Charleston, on King Street, was just a few doors from a gallery owned by George S. Cook (Chapter 2).

In 1883, Barnard settled in Rochester, New York, and there worked with George Eastman, who was developing a new system of film photography. From 1884 to 1886, Barnard operated a studio in Planview, Ohio. He died in 1902 at the age of eighty three.

Barnard's Civil War photographs, particularly those taken during Sherman's campaign of 1864–1865, earned him recognition as one of the most skilled and original craftsmen of his time.

Often overlooked is the fact that he participated in virtually every important photographic development of the nineteenth century. More than simply a Civil War photographer, George Barnard is looked upon today as one of photography's foremost pioneers.

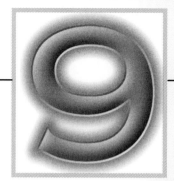

Petersburg and Richmond

In the spring of 1864, as General William T. Sherman's army began its long advance out of Tennessee into Georgia, General Ulysses S. Grant pushed toward Richmond. But whenever Grant made a move, General Robert E. Lee stopped him.

These struggles cost Grant heavily. At Cold Harbor, Virginia, east of Richmond, Grant sent one division after another against Lee's entrenched army. The result was a massacre. Thousands of Northern troops were killed or wounded in a single hour of combat. And nothing was achieved.

Yet Grant would not be stopped. After Cold Harbor, he abruptly pulled his army out of position and ordered a march south across the James River. His ambition now was to capture Petersburg, less than 20 miles south of Richmond.

Petersburg, a key communications and railroad center, was a valuable prize. Railroad tracks fanned out from Petersburg in almost every direction of the compass, linking Richmond, and the entire Confederacy in fact, to the rich farms and orchards of the Shenandoah Valley and to the Atlantic ports that received supplies from Confederate blockade runners. If he could win control of Petersburg, Grant realized, Richmond and perhaps the entire Confederacy might fall.

In setting Petersburg as his target, Grant not only changed his immediate goal; he revised his tactics. This was not to be a quick, decisive battle. Instead, the Northern army, after a few weak and poorly coordinated attacks by their advance units, laid siege to Petersburg.

A siege, according to the dictionary, is "a military blockade of a city or fortified place to compel it to surren-

This famous photograph of General Ulysses S. Grant was taken by one of Mathew Brady's cameramen at Grant's headquarters in Cold Harbor, Virginia, on June 11 or 12, 1864, not long before Grant shifted his army south to begin the siege of Petersburg. Like many of Brady's portrait photographs, it later served as the basis for an engraving (right) that appeared in Harper's Weekly. (Library of Congress; New York Public Library)

der." Grant's struggle for Petersburg was long; it lasted nine and one-half months. And it was persistent, too. While there were periods of relative quiet, the siege involved a long series of brief but extremely violent flare-ups.

As Grant's army took positions south and east of Petersburg, Lee's forces occupied the elaborate fortifications that ringed the city. The summer of 1864 was hot and dry. For men on either side of the battle line, the heat, the dust, and the steady artillery fire made each day agony.

At City Point on the James River, a spur of land just a few miles north and east of Petersburg, Grant established a huge supply center, which became "one of the greatest ports in the world," according to William Frassanito.[1] City Point's long wharves received an unending stream of transports carrying arms and supplies. Troop camps were constructed. Sprawling warehouses sprang up. Hospitals were built at City Point, and Grant established his headquarters there.

Time would turn out to be on Grant's side. As reinforcements poured into City Point, Northern forces came to far outnumber those of the South. And Grant's men were better equipped, better clothed, and better fed, especially when Northern victories elsewhere in the Confederacy cut Lee's lines of supply.

Grant increased the pressure on Lee's defenses by constantly extending the battle line. He ordered his infantrymen to lay down their guns and pick up shovels, and use them to extend the network of trenches farther and farther to the west.

Northern entrenchments eventually covered 30 miles. Opposite this line, the Southern fortifications had to be expanded.

Because Lee's forces were so limited, his defenses were like a rubber band. They could be stretched, but he could not keep stretching them indefinitely. At some point, they would snap.

The winter of 1864–1865 was particularly hard on the Southern soldiers. Food was in short supply, and winter clothing was practically nonexistent. Sickness and disease took a heavy toll.

The end for Lee and the Confederate defenders came in the spring. On March 25, Lee launched a daring assault east of Petersburg and managed to capture Fort Stedman. But Northern forces quickly poured into the area, forcing the Confederates to pull back.

Grant then unleashed an attack of his own below Petersburg. The Confederates counterattacked, but the Northern divisions kept coming. Once the Northern

One of the Confederate soldiers who died in the face of Grant's final assault on Petersburg. This photograph was taken by Thomas C. Roche on April 3, 1865. Within a week after it had been taken, General Lee had surrendered to Grant.
(National Archives)

forces had broken through the Confederate defenses, Grant ordered attacks all along the line of battle. Overwhelmed, the Confederate defenses collapsed.

Lee had no choice but to order a retreat. Grant's army captured Petersburg on April 3. Richmond fell to the Northerners the same day. The long and costly war was drawing to a close.

❖❖❖❖

The struggle at Petersburg provided Civil War cameramen with an unparalleled opportunity to take pho-tographs. So it was that almost every one of the more noted Civil War cameramen appeared at Petersburg at one time or another during the campaign. They made hundreds of photographs—of troops and officers, camps and officers' quarters, trenches and signal towers, and fortifications and bombproof shelters.

Mathew Brady was among the first to arrive. He was at Petersburg for two weeks in June and perhaps for a brief period in July to supervise the photographing of Union forces, artillery crews and generals and their staffs in particular.

Petersburg marked Brady's final battlefield appearance. His plan to become the Civil War's photographic historian was proving more expensive than he ever imagined. By July 1864, he no longer had the money necessary to keep photographic teams in the field. Bills for photographic supplies were going unpaid. Brady could not even pay the rent due on his studio space. By 1868, Brady would be in bankruptcy.

As for Alexander Gardner, after his work at Gettysburg in July 1863, he gave up visiting Civil War battle sites. He remained in Washington to supervise work at his studio and tend to his other business interests.

Gardner named Timothy O'Sullivan to handle operations in the field. O'Sullivan was photographing at Petersburg as early as mid-June, just as Grant's army was getting in position south of the James River.

"While Confederates probed all that winter for weakness in Grant's . . . long line, O'Sullivan searched for pictures," says James D. Horan, a biographer of O'Sullivan. "He was at Fort Hell or Damnation, which was constantly under the fire of sharpshooters in the city. Veterans later recalled it was worth a man's life to expose an inch of his cap."[2] O'Sullivan also photographed in Petersburg after the city's fall.

Photographer John Reekie, who at one time during the war worked for Mathew Brady, took this dramatic photograph of a long line of Union army wagons as they rumbled through Petersburg, on their way to supply Grant's army as it pursued Lee.
(Library of Congress)

Captain Andrew J. Russell was an official army photographer during the Civil War. While much of his time was devoted to taking photographs involving the work of the U. S. Military Railroad Construction Corps, he also visited army encampments and battlegrounds. This is his photograph of Confederate guns captured at Richmond by Grant's army. (National Archives)

Alexander Gardner was the first Northern photographer to enter Richmond after its fall. In this photograph, Gardner depicts the ruins of the Confederate arsenal in Richmond, one of the largest arsenals in the South. To the right are the remains of a Richmond paper mill. (National Archives)

David Knox, another Gardner cameraman, was also active behind the battle lines at Petersburg. A. J. Russell was there in the summer and fall of 1864.

But early in April 1865, when General Grant launched his final assault, neither Russell, Knox, O'Sullivan, nor any member of Brady's team managed to record what took place. Instead, it was left to Thomas C. Roche, who was employed by E. and H. T. Anthony of New York, to photograph the final stages of the Petersburg siege.

For Roche, it was "the chance of a lifetime," says William Frassanito.[3] And Roche made the most of it. His images of Confederate dead are among the most powerful of all the photographs taken at Petersburg.

After the Civil War, Roche continued to work for the Anthony Company, becoming one of the most noted landscape photographers of the day. He traveled the Union Pacific Railroad to California and toured the South, photographing in Georgia, South Carolina, and Florida. During the 1870s, Roche is said to have made more than fifteen thousand negatives.[4]

Shortly after Grant's army marched into Richmond early in April 1865, Alexander Gardner left Washington for the city, becoming the first Northern photographer to arrive upon the scene. Between April 6 and 15, Gardner and his assistants made more than one hundred photographs in Richmond, many of them documenting the terrible destruction that had taken place. About half of the images are believed to have been taken by Gardner himself.[5] Mathew Brady was also on hand at Richmond, directing a team of cameramen.

After the fall of Richmond, Lee retreated westward toward Lynchburg, Virginia, with Grant's army in pursuit. At Sayler's Creek, Union forces overwhelmed the Confederates. The fighting cost Lee about seven thousand casualties, nearly one-third of his army.

Three days later, on April 9, 1865, Lee's Army of Northern Virginia, the men hungry and exhausted, stumbled into Appomattox Courthouse, Virginia. When Union forces cut his line of retreat, Lee realized that it was time to quit, time to end the long and bloody struggle.

Source Notes

Chapter 1
1. Alan Trachtenberg, *Reading American Photographs* (New York: Hill and Wang, 1989), p. 74.
2. Ibid., p. 42.
3. George A. Townsend, "Brady: The Grand Old Man of American Photography," *New York World*, April 12, 1891, p. 26.
4. Trachtenberg, *Reading American Photographs*, p. 94.
5. "The Process of Making a Civil War Photograph," by Douglas Munson, *Incidents of the War*, Vol. 2, No. 2, Summer 1987, p. 7.

Chapter 2
1. Bruce Catton, *The Civil War* (New York: Houghton Mifflin, 1960), p. 23.
2. Jack C. Ramsay, Jr., *Photographer...Under Fire* (Green Bay, Wisconsin: Historical Resources Press, 1994), p. 13.
3. Quoted in Robert Taft, *Photography and the American Scene* (New York: Dover Publications, 1964), p. 478.
4. Ramsey, *Photographer...Under Fire*, p. 16.
5. Ibid., p. 32.
6. Ibid., p. 13.
7. Ibid., p. 116.
8. Ibid., p. 130.
9. Ibid., p. 127.

Chapter 3
1. Stephen M. Forman, *A Guide to Civil War Washington* (Washington, D.C.: Elliott & Clark Publishing, 1995), p. 12.

2. Bruce Catton, *The Civil War* (New York: Houghton Mifflin, 1960), p. 42.
3. Ibid.
4. George A. Townsend, "Brady: The Grand Old Man of American Photography," *New York World*, April 12, 1891, p. 26.
5. Quoted in James D. Horan, *Timothy O'Sullivan, America's Forgotten Photographer* (New York: Doubleday, 1966), p. 34.
6. Ibid., p. 12.
7. Ibid., p. 40.

Chapter 4
1. William C. Davis, editor, *The Guns of '62*, Vol. II, *The Image of War, 1861-1865* (Garden City, New York: Doubleday, 1982), p. 112.
2. Ibid., pp. 112–114.
3. William S. Johnson, *Nineteenth-Century Photography, Annotated Bibliography, 1839–1879* (Boston: G. K. Hall Co., 1990), p. 257.
4. Josephine Cobb, "*Mathew B. Brady's Photographic Gallery in Washington*," Columbia Historical Society Records [c. 1955], pp. 29–34, 36.

Chapter 5
1. Quoted from James V. Murfin, *The Gleam of Bayonets: The Battle of Antietam and the Maryland Campaign of 1862* (New York: Thomas Yoseloff, 1965), p. 25.
2. William C. Davis, *The Battlefields of the Civil War* (London: Salamander Books, 1991), p. 85.

3. William A. Frassanito, *Antietam: The Photographic Legacy of America's Bloodiest Day* (New York: Charles Scribner's Sons, 1978), p. 17.
4. Ibid., p. 76.
5. Ibid.
6. Ibid., p. 52.
7. Ibid., p. 53.
8. "Brady's Photographs, Pictures of the Dead," *New York Times*, October 20, 1862, p. 5.
9. "The Battle of Antietam," *Harper's Weekly*, October 18, 1862, p. 663.

Chapter 6
1. Constance Sullivan, editor, *Landscapes of the Civil War* (New York: Alfred A. Knopf, 1995), p. 18.
2. Dorothy Meserve Kunhardt and Philip B. Kunhardt, Jr., *Mathew Brady and His World* (Alexandria, Virginia: Time-Life Books, 1977), p. 52.
3. Ross J. Kelbaugh, *Introduction to Civil War Photography* (Gettysburg, Pennsylvania: Thomas Publications, 1991), p. 11.
4. Ibid., p. 19.
5. Ibid., p. 27.

Chapter 7
1. William C. Davis, *The Battlefields of the Civil War* (London: Salamander Books, 1995), p. 163.
2. Ibid., p. 175.
3. Ibid.

4. William A. Frassanito, *Gettysburg: A Journey in Time* (New York: Charles Scribner's Sons, 1975), p. 31.
5. Ibid., pp. 35, 36.
6. "Reminiscences of Gettysburg," *Harper's Weekly*, August 23, 1863, p. 534.
7. Frassanito, *Gettysburg: A Journey in Time*, pp. 47, 48.
8. Brooks Johnson, *An Enduring Interest: The Photographs of Alexander Gardner* (Norfolk, Virginia: Chrysler Museum, 1991), p. 36.

Chapter 8
1. Quoted in Mark M. Boatner III, *The Civil War Dictionary* (New York: Vintage Books, 1991), p. 30.
2. William C. Davis, editor, *The Image of War*, Vol. VI, *The End of an Era* (Garden City, New York: Doubleday, 1982), p. 146.
3. Bruce Catton, *The Civil War* (Boston: Houghton Mifflin, 1988), p. 235.
4. William C. Davis, *The End of an Era*, p. 162.
5. Keith F. Davis, *George N. Barnard, Photographer of Sherman's Campaign* (Kansas City, Missouri: Hallmark Cards, 1990), pp. 21-2.
6. Quoted in Michael L. Carlebach, *The Origins of Photojournalism in America* (Washington: Smithsonian Institution Press, 1992), p. 42.
7. Ibid.
8. Ibid., p. 78.
9. George N. Barnard, *Photographic Views of Sherman's Campaign*. Republication of the edition originally pub-

lished in 1866. (New York: Dover Publications, 1982), p. iii.
10. Ibid., p. vi.

Chapter 9
1. William A. Frassanito, *Grant and Lee: The Virginia Campaigns* (Gettysburg: Thomas Publications, 1983), p. 268.
2. James D. Horan, *Timothy O'Sullivan, America's Forgotten Photographer* (New York: Doubleday, 1966), p. 49.
3. Frassanito, *Grant and Lee: The Virginia Campaigns*, p. 343.
4. William S. Johnson, *Nineteenth Century Photography: An Annotated Bibliography* (Boston: G. K. Hall Co., 1990), p. 520.
5. Frassanito, *Grant and Lee: The Virginia Campaigns*, p. 379.

To learn more about Mathew Brady and his work, you can read another book by George Sullivan, *Mathew Brady: His Life and Photographs*, published by Dutton's Children's Books in 1994.

Another source of information on Civil War photography is the Library of Congress National Digital Library, currently available online at:

http://lcweb2.loc.gov/ammem/cwphome.html

This site includes Selected Civil War Photographs from the Library of Congress, 1861–1865. More than 1,000 photographs can be accessed, along with biographical information on Mathew Brady, a description of the process of taking photographs at the time of the Civil War, search tips, and a technical note on photographs from this period.

Index

Page numbers in *italics* refer to illustrations.